LIFE STORIES

MARTIN LUTHER KING JR.

Gillian Gosman

PowerKiDS press

New York

Published in 2011 by The Rosen Publishing Group, Inc.
29 East 21st Street, New York, NY 10010

First Edition

Editor: Jennifer Way
Book Design: Ashley Burrell and Erica Clendening

Photo Credits: Cover (inset) Ernst Haas/Getty Images; cover (background), pp. 16–17, 19 Hulton Archive/ Getty Images; pp. 4–5 Walter Bennett/Time & Life Pictures/Getty Images; p. 6 Travel Ink/Getty Images; pp. 6–7, 17, 22 (center) AFP/Getty Images; p. 8 Marion Post Wolcott/Library of Congress/Getty Images; pp. 8–9 © Dinodia/age fotostock; pp. 10–11 Donald Uhrbrock/Time & Life Pictures/Getty Images; p. 11 Library of Congress; pp. 12, 12–13, 22 (top) Don Cravens/Time & Life Pictures/Getty Images; p. 14 Rolls Press/ Popperfoto/Getty Images; pp. 14–15 Francis Miller/Time & Life Pictures/Getty Images; pp. 18–19 Michael Ochs Archives/Getty Images; pp. 20–21 Lynn Pelham/Time & Life Pictures/Getty Images.

Library of Congress Cataloging-in-Publication Data

Gosman, Gillian.
  Martin Luther King Jr. / by Gillian Gosman. — 1st ed.
      p. cm. — (Life stories)
  Includes index.
  ISBN 978-1-4488-2583-7 (library binding) — ISBN 978-1-4488-2755-8 (pbk.) —
ISBN 978-1-4488-2756-5 (6-pack)
  1. King, Martin Luther, Jr., 1929-1968—Juvenile literature. 2. African Americans—Biography—Juvenile literature. 3. Civil rights workers—United States—Biography—Juvenile literature. 4. Baptists—United States—Clergy—Biography—Juvenile literature. 5. African Americans—Civil rights—History—20th century—Juvenile literature. I. Title.
  E185.97.K5G665 2011
  323.092—dc22
  [B]
                                     2010034357

Manufactured in the United States of America
CPSIA Compliance Information: Batch #WW11PK: For Further Information contact Rosen Publishing, New York, New York at 1-800-237-9932

Contents

Meet Martin Luther King Jr.

On the third Monday in January, we **celebrate** Martin Luther King Jr. Day. Schools, public offices, and many businesses are closed. Who was Martin Luther King Jr., though?

Martin Luther King Jr. was a civil rights leader. He was famous for his powerful speeches.

King was a **pastor** and **civil rights** leader. He was also a writer. He wrote six books. King believed America was a place where people of different races would one day live together peacefully and with equal rights.

YOUNG MARTIN

Martin Luther King Jr. was born on January 15, 1929, in Atlanta, Georgia. His father was a pastor. His mother was very active in his church.

This is King's birthplace in Atlanta.

In 1964, at 35, King was awarded the Nobel Peace Prize. He was the youngest man to receive the award.

Martin did so well in school that he entered Morehouse College, in Atlanta, at 15! He **graduated** from Morehouse in 1948. He went on to study **religion** at Crozer Theological Seminary, in Pennsylvania, and then at Boston University.

Life in Segregated America

King lived in a time of **segregation**. Segregation laws kept blacks and whites separated in every possible way. Blacks and whites even had to use different public bathrooms. Blacks who broke segregation laws could be arrested.

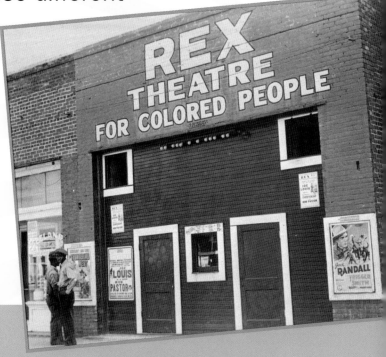

This photo shows a movie theater for African Americans in Mississippi.

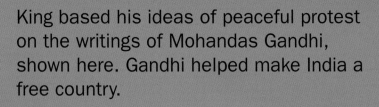

King based his ideas of peaceful protest on the writings of Mohandas Gandhi, shown here. Gandhi helped make India a free country.

In the 1950s, civil rights **activists** wanted to show people segregation was wrong. To do this, activists sometimes **boycotted**, or stayed away from, businesses. They also **protested**, or acted out, peacefully.

A Life in the Church

In 1948, King was **ordained** as a Baptist minister. On June 18, 1953, he married Coretta Scott. The following year, he finished his schooling and took a job as pastor of the Dexter Avenue Baptist Church in Montgomery, Alabama.

Here is King at home with his wife, Coretta, and two of their four children, Yolanda and Martin Luther King III.

This is the Dexter Avenue Baptist Church in Montgomery. King was the pastor there from 1954 until 1960.

As pastor there, King was an important and well-known member of Montgomery's African-American community. He became a leader of the city's growing civil rights movement.

TAKING IT TO THE STREETS

In late 1955, blacks in Montgomery were angry about segregation on the city's buses. King was one of the leaders who helped Montgomery's black community boycott the city buses.

King is standing next to a Montgomery city bus shortly after the boycott ended on December 20, 1956.

The boycott began on December 1, 1955. It lasted more than a year, until Alabama's bus segregation laws were changed. The Montgomery bus boycott was a big win for the civil rights movement.

COMING TOGETHER

In 1957, King and other civil rights activists formed the Southern Christian Leadership Conference, or SCLC. The group organized African-American churches and their members in the fight for civil rights.

The people in this picture are having a sit-in to protest segregated bus waiting rooms in the South.

Here King is speaking to a group of civil rights activists at a protest.

The SCLC planned marches, sit-ins, and other peaceful protests throughout the South. King and other activists were often put in jail, sprayed with fire hoses, or beaten by police for these protests.

THE MARCH ON WASHINGTON

On August 28, 1963, King and the other civil rights leaders marched on Washington, D.C. More than 250,000 marchers walked from the Washington Monument to the Lincoln Memorial that day.

The people who took part in the March on Washington filled this park called the National Mall.

King gave his "I have a dream" speech from the steps of the Lincoln Memorial.

It was at the Lincoln Memorial that King gave his famous "I have a dream" speech. This speech was shown on television and brought King's message into homes across America.

Making It Law

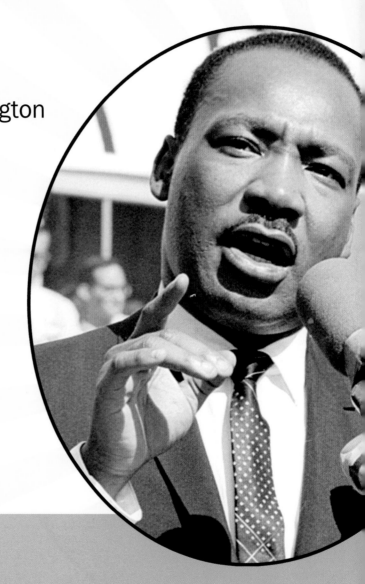

The March on Washington sent a strong message. Soon after the march, Congress passed two important civil rights laws. These were the Civil Rights Act of 1964 and the National Voting Rights Act of 1965.

King's leadership helped bring about advances in civil rights for all Americans.

President Lyndon B. Johnson (center) is shaking King's hand after signing the Civil Rights Act into law.

The Civil Rights Act made segregation illegal. The National Voting Rights Act said that states must allow every citizen to sign up to vote.

KILLED IN MEMPHIS

On April 4, 1968, King was standing on a balcony at the Lorraine Motel in Memphis, Tennessee. James Earl Ray shot King from a nearby building. King died an hour later.

People across the country were sad about King's death. Thousands of people came to his funeral in Atlanta, shown here.

King's **assassination** was met with sadness and anger across the country. King's followers called for peace. King's message of nonviolence lived on. This is one of the reasons his life is marked by a holiday each January.

TIMELINE

January 15, 1929

Martin Luther King Jr. is born in Atlanta.

1955–1956

The Montgomery bus boycott is held.

King and other civil rights leaders hold the March on Washington.

August 28, 1963

April 4, 1968

King is assassinated in Memphis.

1965

The National Voting Rights Act is passed.

1964

The Civil Rights Act is passed.

Glossary

activists (AK-tih-vists) People who take action for what they believe is right.

assassination (uh-sa-suh-NAY-shun) The killing of an important person.

boycotted (BOY-kot-ed) Refused to deal with a person, nation, or business.

celebrate (SEH-leh-brayt) To honor an important moment by doing special things.

civil rights (SIH-vul RYTS) The rights that citizens have. The civil rights movement is the groups and people who worked toward equality for all.

graduated (GRA-jeh-wayt-ed) To have finished a course of school.

ordained (or-DAYND) Gave someone a position in a church as a preacher.

pastor (PAS-ter) A minister in a church.

protested (PROH-test-ed) Acted out in disagreement of something.

religion (rih-LIH-jen) A belief in and a way of honoring a god or gods.

segregation (seh-grih-GAY-shun) The act of keeping people of one race, sex, or social class away from others.

Index

A

activists, 9, 14–15

Atlanta, Georgia,
6–7, 22

B

blacks, 8, 12

businesses, 4, 9

C

church(es), 6, 10,
14

Crozer Theological
Seminary, 7

F

father, 6

L

laws, 8, 13, 18

leader(s), 5, 11–12,
16, 22

M

Martin Luther King Jr.
Day, 4

minister, 10

Morehouse College,
7

P

pastor, 5–6,
10–11

Pennsylvania, 7

R

races, 5

religion, 7

rights, 5, 14

S

school(s), 4, 7

segregation, 8–9,
12, 19

Web Sites

Due to the changing nature of Internet links, PowerKids Press has developed
an online list of Web sites related to the subject of this book. This site is
updated regularly. Please use this link to access the list:
www.powerkidslinks.com/life/mlking/